SECURITY 101

written by

Eric O. Parker, B.S. Security Management

TABLE OF CONTENTS

INTRODUCTION

This training module will define and discuss Security Patrol issues and tactics. We will cover topics including professional appearance and conduct, safety, and customer service. While the laws in your state, county, and city may differ, we will reference California professional and penal codes and statistics from the U.S. Bureau of Labor Statistics.

It has been said that paperwork is the bane of law enforcement's existence. It doesn't have to be!

Computerization of the documents that keep us in line may have streamlined the effort, but the basics have not changed.

This training module will help you to remain organized in every step of the report writing process, from observation to note taking to documenting evidence and the report itself.

We will cover witness statements and photography. as well as easy to remember guides for recalling and describing cars and people.

We will also cover courtroom demeanor and how to appear in court successfully and professionally.

This training module will define and discuss Loss Prevention issues and tactics. We will cover legal issues such as criminal and civil liability and how to protect yourself. We will also define the differences between internal and external theft, methods for evidence collection, investigative techniques and tactics, emergency situations, and basic reporting standards for loss prevention.

DIRECTIVES

Security patrol is one of the most common duties any security officer carries out. Security departments tend to assign their staff in the manner that police and sheriff's departments assign the majority of their personnel to patrol an assigned area. Whether it's one building, a parking lot, a mall, or an apartment complex, the basic functions and purposes are the same. The primary functions for any patrol situation are:

1) Prevent criminal activity and/or safety hazards.

    a) as a visible deterrent

    b) actively interfering with or interrupting criminal acts

    c) training clients or customers in safety

    d) removing items that may cause safety hazards to a safer location.

2) Make accurate observations of conditions and situations that could not be prevented.

    a) maintain accurate notes.

    b) use a digital camera when allowed.

    c) use digital voice and/or video equipment when allowed.

    d) log and maintain accurate records of all encounters with people outside your department.

3) Report said observations to the appropriate entities in a timely manner (accurately and thoroughly)

    a) your supervisor or director

    b) client contact

    c) law enforcement or other government agencies as deemed appropriate by your superiors.

4) Assist in restoring normalcy when possible.

    a) accept direction from the agency that assumes command over any emergency situation.

    b) remain within the scope of your department's policies.

5) DO NOT INTERFERE with outside agencies.

    (a) Even if you are temporarily deputized (assigned specific duties by an on-duty sworn peace officer to assist with his or her investigation into a crime) you are not a peace officer by definition.

    (b) A sworn peace officer is "any person who comes within the provisions of this chapter and who otherwise meets all standards imposed by law on a peace officer is a peace officer..." (CA Penal code 830"

Patrol officers are often the first persons to respond to an emergency, but more importantly they are ambassadors for the entire security department or firm, as the case may be. You represent more than just yourself; you represent your employer and your clientele. Your professional appearance and mannerism will often dictate the mood of every contact you make with the public, consensual or otherwise. Will those contacts start and end on positive notes, or will they go badly? Most of the time this is up to you.

"To Protect and Serve" is the motto of the Los Angeles Police Department, as memorialized on TV's *DRAGNET.* The Sacramento County Sheriff's Department patrol vehicles boast a similar slogan, "Service With Concern."

The State of California clearly defines the roles of security officers via the Bureau of Security and Investigative Services (a division of the Department of Consumer Affairs) as follows; to PREVENT, OBSERVE, and REPORT. However, Loss Prevention Agents have a slightly different set of directives, PREVENT, APPREHEND, and RECOVER.

1) PREVENT criminal activity and safety hazards.

2) RECOVER stolen property.

3) APPREHEND criminal offenders if possible AND safe to attempt.

Your store is not in the habit of giving away its products or goods and services. They what to exchange them for money. This is how they make profits and pay their expenses, such as land & building leases, utilities, maintaining their inventory, payroll, taxes, and other expenses. The loss of their property or cash cuts into this ability.

Why do we refer to your post as "your store" when you certainly do not own it? We find that when we take a stronger sense of pride in ownership of out patrol beat, our area of concern or our clientele and we feel a greater sense of pride in accomplishment in our daily activities,

We tackle our duties with the knowledge that the criminals we apprehend and safety issues we address make our place of business a safer environment. This sense of ownership ought to empower you with a greater sense of responsibility.

PROFESSIONALISM

How many times have you heard the expression "dress for the occasion" or "dress for success" in the past? Those concepts apply to Loss Prevention Agents in the same ways that maintaining a clean, well-pressed uniform and a proper haircut and grooming standards apply to law enforcement and security officers. We have to fit in with the clientele at each work site. High-end retail outlets and the average discount clothier each cater to different looking shoppers, as well as shoplifters and staff. We need to blend in and mingle.

This does not mean that we can afford to wear our pants below the waist (as is so popular with many people) or to keep our shoes untied or wear flip flops.

Chrysler Motor Company had a slogan in the 1980's that suggested that "form follows function" in their products, which works perfectly for cars and trucks, however it does not always allow professional Loss Prevention Agents the ability to perform their functions adequately. We are carrying handcuffs, a two-way radio or cellular telephone, and some form of readily accessible Loss Prevention identification while on duty, and we may need to get to any or all of these items with little or no warning.

We also find ourselves in potentially violent situations, again with little or no warning, and when your stylishly worn pants fall down your suspect will either get away or overtake you. Neither situation will yield a favorable outcome. If you dress for success in the first place you can avoid these unacceptable circumstances.

IS THIS JOB FOR ME?

Take the time to observe the clientele in your new place of employment before you get started. Ask yourself the following questions as you prepare for your new position as a Loss Prevention Agent:

1) What do the clientele commonly wear?

    a) You may want to modify your working wardrobe accordingly.

    b) You may not want to look like you are out of place when not in uniform.

    c) Consider the following.

        i)   comfortable jeans or khakis,

        ii)   shoes that will be comfortable for up to 12 hours per shift

        iii)   a clean over-shirt, or hoodie or sports coat (as appropriate for your store)

            (1) this will help to conceal your ID, radio and other necessary equipment.

        iv)   Facial hair or exposed tattoos (again, as appropriate for your store)

2) How do the common clients conduct themselves?

3) Do you know many of them personally?

a) This may be a good reason to NOT take this particular assignment.

b) No one wants to arrest their friends or family or be referred to negatively by their friends or family for arresting another friend of theirs.

While you need to fit in, you also need to be able to immediately return to the role of a security or loss prevention professional when confronting a suspect and when approaching management with a safety concern.

RESPONSIBILITIES

1) To safeguard lives and property.

2) To protect the peaceful against violence or disorder

3) To respect the Constitutional rights of all to liberty, equality and justice.

4) I will be exemplary in obeying the law and the regulations of my department.

5) I will cooperate with all legally authorized agencies and their representatives in the pursuit of justice.

6) I will enforce the law courteously and appropriately without fear or favor, malice or ill will, never employing unnecessary force or violence and never accepting gratuities.

7) I will never act outrageously or permit my personal feelings, prejudices, political beliefs, aspirations, animosities or friendships to influence my decisions.

8) I will never engage in acts of corruption or bribery, nor will I condone such acts by other Loss Prevention Agents.

9) I know that I alone am responsible for my own standard of professional performance and will take every

reasonable opportunity to enhance and improve my level of knowledge and competence.

10)I recognize the position I hold is a symbol of professional faith, and I accept it as a professional trust to be held so long as I am true to these ethics.

CUSTOMER SERVICE

Everything we do as security professionals can be summed up as customer service. Whether patrolling a shopping mall or guarding a parking lot, warehouse, casino, amusement park, or home owner's association from intrusion, the basic concept is the same; we are there at the request of the client (or employer as the case may be), and as such we are expected to perform our duties at their behest.

When I was in charge of security for a major hotel in Nevada, that corporate entity had a strict policy of always saying "yes" to their guests' requests. Security was the only department with authorization to say "no". Sometimes you have to upset the customer or client in order to carry out your duties.

This does not excuse or endorse any lapse in courtesy. On the contrary, we must remain respectful of everyone we meet. Everyone has certain rights in this country, and even though we do not always work for or represent the government, as professionals we need to respect everyone's rights as we do.

SECURITY CODE OF ETHICS

As a security professional it is my duty to adhere to the following ethical standards at all times:

1) To safeguard lives and property.

2) To protect the peaceful against violence or disorder

3) To respect the Constitutional rights of all to liberty, equality and justice.

4) I will be exemplary in obeying the law and the regulations of my department.

5) I will cooperate with all legally authorized agencies and their representatives in the pursuit of justice.

6) I will enforce the law courteously and appropriately without fear or favor, malice or ill will, never employing unnecessary force or violence and never accepting gratuities.

7) I will never act outrageously or permit my personal feelings, prejudices, political beliefs, aspirations, animosities or friendships to influence my decisions.

8) I will never engage in acts of corruption or bribery, nor will I condone such acts by other Loss Prevention Agents.

9) I know that I alone am responsible for my own standard of professional performance and will take every reasonable opportunity to enhance and improve my level of knowledge and competence.

10)I recognize the position I hold is a symbol of professional faith, and I accept it as a professional trust to be held so long as I am true to these ethics.

It may sound strange to think that there is a specific code of ethics for security officers, and that it might ever have anything to do with patrol tactics and techniques.

Your ethical behavior, or lack thereof, absolutely can and should determine how the course of events that will unfold during your assigned shift will turn out. Security professionals must be mentally and emotionally prepared to accept that their conduct will be filmed and that someone might try to use that against them. If we remain vigilant in our ethical conduct those videos will exonerate us from criminal or civil liability. Protect yourself from yourself as well as from other people or entities.

PROFESSIONAL APPEARANCE

As noted earlier, your physical presence and professional appearance can be all the deterrent necessary to maintain a relatively safe and secure environment. Keep your uniform clean and reasonably wrinkle free. Wear the entire uniform with pride.

Many departments address grooming and jewelry issues, so stick with your employer's or client's requirements. I suggest the following list in the event your department has not yet addressed these issues:

1) Maintain appropriate hairstyles and makeup (if worn)

2) Bathe prior to going on duty.

a) Use a mild but effective deodorant, or similar product.

b) Smelling nice is one thing, smelling strong is another.

3) Try to keep your jewelry to a minimum.

a) This is for your safety.

b) Dangling earrings or other visible pierced jewelry can be pulled or forcibly removed, causing pain or injury to yourself or other persons.

c) Multiple rings and bracelets can also cause unintentional injury or harm.

4) If it clashes with your uniform then it doesn't belong on your uniform. This applies to t-shirts and footwear as well as outer wear. If your department does not yet supply appropriate outerwear, suggest that they do so to maintain a professional appearance for the entire department.

SAFETY

As stated on the back cover, I have always trained my officers to remain safe and courteous at all times. Not only do I subscribe to law and order, but I have a specific set of rules that I have used in my daily life, especially in security. Those rules include, but are not limited to:

1) At the end of your shift be sure you go home alive.

    a) preferably without a visit to the hospital

2) Remain respectful of everyone you encounter, regardless of why you're meeting.

    a) "sir" or "ma'am" at all times

    b) do not cuss or use vulgar language or gestures, except as direct quotes in your report and notebook.

3) We do not accept tips, gratuities, or bribes.

4) Everything you say and do while on duty is being recorded by someone, whether you know it or not, so act accordingly.

Rule number 4 has been the hardest to accept. I got into this business in 1991 in a small town in Northern California. Cell phones came in bags and digital cameras were basically unheard of back then. Now both are combined, and nearly everyone has one.

STAY SAFE!

EXTERNAL THEFT

External Theft occurs when a customer or patron of the store or shopping center or retail outlet that you (the Loss Prevention Agent) are guarding removes items belonging to the store (or another patron inside the store) without permission or due compensation (they did not pay for said items in an agreed upon business transaction).

We have an image of people dressed all in black, often form-fitting outfits and ski-masks, working only in the dead of night when we think of burglars. The fact of the matter is those movie stereotypical burglars are simple fiction. This being said, should you observe a person or group of people dressed in this sort of garb entering your store, it may be safe to assume that crimes worse than burglary are imminent. Stay alert!

California defines entering a structure with the intent of stealing or committing another felony once inside as burglary, as discussed in the Use of Force section of this manual. The CA penal code section 459 (the burglary statute) will be the primary charge listed in your report when you arrest a person for stealing or shoplifting from your store.

1) If a person (s) enters your store, selects a victim, then murders said victim, have they also committed burglary? YES

2) If a person (s) enters your store, selects a victim, then attempts to kidnap said victim, have they also committed burglary? YES

3) If a person (s) enters your store, selects a pair of cheap earrings, and takes them without paying for them, have they also committed burglary? YES

The petty theft of the cheap earrings, or shoplifting, may be a misdemeanor crime, but they are stealing from your store, the primary qualifying factor in a burglary charge. Remember, it's not only the theft or the value of the stolen property, or even the other felony crime (s) committed that make the case for burglary, but the fact that the would-be thief entered the store with the intent to steal or commit some other crime makes the crime of burglary a fact to be proven in court.

How do we prove intent? A confession works perfectly. Sudden utterances when your suspect is approached or apprehended caught on audio recorders makes this stand up in court. If you are not yet in the habit of recording every encounter you make, we encourage you to do so. We will discuss this further in the Apprehension & Detention section of this module.

A cursory search for weapons (allowable when arresting or detaining a suspect, *TERRY v. Ohio*) may reveal a concealed weapon in your suspect's possession. We can reasonably infer that the suspect intended to use the weapon to intimidate or threaten your store's staff into complying with a demand to surrender money or other items, or to deter pursuit or arrest by Loss Prevention Agents or other store staff. This fits California's definition of a robbery (CA Penal Code 211, the taking of another's property from his/her possession or immediate presence accomplished by force or fear), which in turn provides evidence that your subject has committed the crime of burglary.

An inventory of your detainee's property (this MUST not be confused with a search of his/her property) may yield additional stolen property, possession of possible contraband items, or evidence of additional criminal activity. Regardless of what your detainee has in their possession, your only purpose here is to lay it out on a clean surface, photograph and catalog it, then collect it (WEAR GLOVES!) to be turned over to law enforcement (with a copy of the inventory, not the original, the original goes with your report) when they take custody of your detainee. This will save you from losing your house or car during a civil liability lawsuit later.

INTERNAL THEFT

Another duty for Loss Prevention Agents is to prevent, detect, and report internal theft. Internal theft is exactly like external theft, except that instead of looking at customers and patrons, you are looking at employees and management.

Internal Theft occurs when an employee or manager of the store / shopping center / retail outlet that you (the Loss Prevention Agent) are guarding removes items belonging to the store (or another patron inside the store) without permission or due compensation (they did not pay for said items in an agreed upon business transaction).

Internal Theft happens for a number of reasons. Maybe the employee feels they are not being paid adequately, or that they were somehow wronged by management. Regardless of why they decided to steal, they obviously formed the intent to commit a crime or they likely never would have taken the store's property without permission in the first place.

California defines entering a structure with the intent of stealing or committing another felony once inside as burglary, as discussed in the Use of Force section of this manual. The CA penal code section 459 (the burglary statute) will be the primary charge listed in your report when you arrest a person for stealing or shoplifting from your store.

    1) If an employee enters your store, selects a victim, then murders said victim, have they also committed burglary? YES

    2) If an employee enters your store, selects a victim, then attempts to kidnap said victim, have they also committed burglary? YES

    How do we prove intent? A confession works perfectly. Sudden utterances when approached or apprehended caught on audio recorders makes this stand up in court. If you are not yet in the habit of recording every encounter you make, we encourage you to do so..

    Many disgruntled employees will confess when apprehended, mostly because they really just want to make their point known to the people they feel wronged them.

    A cursory search for weapons (allowable when arresting or detaining a subject, *TERRY v. Ohio*) may reveal a concealed weapon in the employee's possession. We can reasonably infer that the subject intended to use the weapon to intimidate or threaten your store's management or owner. We will discuss this further in the Apprehension & Detention section of this manual. This fits California's definition of kidnapping, false imprisonment is the unlawful violation of the personal liberty of another (CA PC 236). Again, we see a felony crime that meets the secondary requirement for a burglary charge.

An inventory of your detainee's property (this MUST not be confused with a search of his/her property) may yield additional stolen property, possession of possible contraband items, or evidence of additional criminal activity. Regardless of what your detainee has in their possession, your only purpose here is to lay it out on a clean surface, photograph and catalog it, then collect it (WEAR GLOVES!) to be turned over to law enforcement (with a copy of the inventory, not the original, the original goes with your report) when they take custody of your detainee. This will save you from losing your house or car during a civil liability lawsuit later.

According to California law, you act in lawful self-defense if you:

1) reasonably believe that you are in imminent danger of being killed, seriously injured, or unlawfully touched,

2) believe that immediate force is necessary to prevent that danger, and

3) use no more force than necessary to defend against that danger.

California self-defense law justifies your injuring (or even using deadly force) another person if these conditions are satisfied. This means that if these requirements are met, self-defense can serve as a complete defense to a California violent crime if you are forced to kill or injure another.

It should be noted that California self-defense law not only protects you against attacks from people, but also from animals. If you defend yourself against imminent danger coming from a dog attack, for example, any reasonable measures you take to protect yourself will be excused.

If only some of these requirements are met, you may still be able to reduce your criminal liability under the theory of imperfect self-defense (which is discussed in the following section).

The prosecutor has the burden of proving beyond a reasonable doubt that the killing or other alleged injury that you inflicted on another was unlawful. With respect to proving that your actions were only executed in self-defense, there are two options:

1) you may choose to testify or otherwise actively present evidence that you acted in self-defense, or

2) the court will instruct the jury on its own motion (legally known as "sua sponte") if the evidence supports the fact that your acts were performed in self-defense.

The three most important facts that must be proven under California self-defense law are:

1) that the danger or threat was imminent,

2) that you reasonably believed you would be harmed, and

3) that you reasonably responded to that danger.

REASONABLE RESPONSE

The general rule under California self-defense law is that you are only allowed to use enough force to combat the force being used against you.

However, if you have previously been threatened by your attacker, you are entitled to act more quickly and with more force than someone who has not been threatened. Deadly force, however, may only be justified if you are about to suffer great bodily injury or death and if there is no other alternative.

Similarly, while you are permitted to defend against force being used against you, you are not permitted to act out of vengeance. However, you are entitled to stand your ground until your safety is no longer threatened. Once you have secured your safety, you must cease fighting or you lose your right to claim this privilege.

Note that even if you are the aggressor in the fight, which typically precludes you from asserting self-defense, you may plead self-defense if:

1) you make a good faith effort to stop fighting and clearly indicate that you are trying to do so (but the other party doesn't stop fighting), or

2) the other party counters your initial non deadly attack with deadly force.

Although some states require that you retreat before responding to force with force, California self-defense law does not. In fact, even if you think you may face a deadly attack by, for example, going somewhere you know an enemy frequently hangs out, and are subsequently compelled to act in self-defense, you are still permitted to go to that location.

However, you are not permitted to seek a fight with the intent to create a real or illusory threat necessity to act in self-defense.

USE OF FORCE

I sincerely hope that you never have to, in the course of your duties or your personal life, find yourself in a position where you have to use physically force in defense of your own or someone else's life. While this is one of your fundamental duties it should not become an objective you look forward to. Physical altercations always result in someone getting hurt, and you could be the one hurting, or worse.

According to the Bureau of Labor Statistics (BLS), there are approximately 1,028,830 security officers or guards employed in the United States. 63 of those officers' lost their lives while in the course of their duties, either to industrial accidents, health issues, or other incidents in their workplaces. There were 12,500 non-fatal injuries and illnesses reported.

The National Institute of Justice (NIJ) suggests that any excessive use of force is any level of force applied that exceeds the amount of force any reasonable, similarly trained individual would use in a given situation. Since every situation will be unique there cannot be a universal response to any two or more situations. The closest we can hope to get to a universal response is to remain professional and prepared.

Every security or loss prevention department should have a specific policy in place for the use of force while on duty. Some departments absolutely forbid physical contact while on duty, while others prefer a more hand-on approach. Pay close attention to your department's policies. What follows here is a suggested guideline and is in no way suggestive that any department's policies are incorrect or inadequate.

1) Your professional appearance and **physical presence** will deter a large portion of incidents and safety hazards with no further contact or action necessary.

2) Using a clear, and sometimes loud, **command voice prompt** to prevent or stop criminal or unruly activity works in many situations, often resulting in an apology from the offender r the offender fleeing the incident scene.

3) The use of **directional control** is where we may have to point casually and courteously someone in the correct direction. One such method would be to gently, with an open hand, touch and guide someone by their upper arm to explain where they are supposed to be. Respect is something we can only demand from ourselves, so in the event pointing and telling someone

where they need to be we must remain courteous when physically redirecting someone.

   a) Remember to deescalate the situational response as soon as possible. Once order has been restored there is no need for additional or continued force.

   4) Continued resistance can result the deployment of more forceful hand techniques, including a **physical arrest with restraints**. Check with your state and local laws, and always adhere to your department's policies regarding physically arresting any persons.

   a) Remember to deescalate the situational response as soon as possible. Once order has been restored there is no need for additional or continued force. At this level you are risking your own employment status, possibly your own freedom, if you do not deescalate.

   5) **Non-lethal or less-than-lethal weapons** may be necessary in response to a violent subject or subjects. This includes chemical sprays, stun guns, tasers, and impact batons. While these weapons are designed for self-defense, and are generally considered to be non-lethal, the inappropriate deployment of any of these weapons can result in unintentional loss of life.

a) If you have not been trained and certified in the use of these or similar items, or the use of same is prohibited by your department or state, do not use them at all. Take appropriate measures to maintain your own safety and refer the situation to local law enforcement.

b) Remember to deescalate the situational response as soon as possible. Once order has been restored there is no need for additional or continued force.

6) The use of **lethal force** is acceptable only in the event that it is absolutely necessary to prevent loss of life or sexual assault upon yourself or another person, and no other reasonable course of action will likely have the same result regarding said attempted or in progress crime.

a) If you have not been trained and certified in the use deadly force weapons (firearms), or the use of same is prohibited by your department or state, do not use them at all. Take appropriate measures to maintain your own safety and refer the situation to local law enforcement.

b) Remember to deescalate the situational response as soon as possible. Once order has been restored there is no need for additional or continued force.

I cannot stress enough the importance of adhering to this or a similar use of force continuum. De-escalation immediately after any incident arises where any use of force became necessary is as important to restoring normalcy as it is to officer safety. Document every event, in the exact order it occurred, as accurately as possible.

Your notes will not only help you assemble an accurate incident report and statement for law enforcement, but they are expected to appear in court with you when subpoenaed. Maintain your notebook in a clean and clear manner and retain it for future reference for at least five years, even after your employment concludes. You never know when a case will actually go to court, and those notebooks can be the difference between determining if you acted legally or not, and whether or not you can be held civilly accountable for your actions.

STAY SAFE!

REPORTS / STATEMENTS

Accuracy in your reports will make or break your case for you. It could also relieve you from having to testify when the defense concedes and settles for a reduced sentence or restitution based on your abundance of accurate evidence.

Write every report like it Is going to court because it will and so will you. Take your time and remember the ABC's of report writing:

1) Accurate

   a) Make certain that every known and verifiable detail is included:

      (i) Identify yourself, your employer and store site, your victim and your suspect.

      (ii) Identify what the exact nature if the incident is (theft, assault, accident, etc. and include penal codes when applicable).

      (iii) Articulate how you became aware of the theft or incident.

      (iv) Articulate how the property was taken, when, and if you know and can prove it, who stole it.

(v) Tell your readers how you apprehended the suspect and / or how you recovered the property (a separate report may be necessary to articulate the use of force, if any occurred).

(vi) Tell your readers who you contacted to report the situation to.

(2) Law Enforcement

(3) Store Management

(4) Your Supervisor or Watch Commander

b) Articulate what the final disposition of this case is:

(i) Was medical attention requested or required, and if so, administered properly?

(ii) Was any safety hazard tended to properly, and by whom?

(iii) Was your suspect taken into custody to be booked into jail or juvenile hall by law enforcement, or cited and released?

(iv) Was the property recovered returned to its owner or secured by law enforcement as evidence?

2) Brief

    a) This is your time to tell your story. You are NOT writing the great American novel. More is not always better. One way to keep this concept in mind is to remember the K.I.S.S. method:

        (i) Keep It Simple Stupid (this is not to insult anyone. The "Stupid" part is meant to make you smile and make this method easier to remember.)

        (ii) It helps to assume that you are writing your report so that an average 15 year old can easily understand it.

        (iii) Avoid the three dollar words.

        (iv) Use proper grammar and spelling.

        (v) Separate your thoughts into individual paragraphs.

        (vi) When you change subjects or thoughts, skip a line and start a new paragraph. This may increase your total number of pages but it can also reduce the likelihood that you will have to explain your report to the District Attorney, Defense Attorney or a jury or your superiors.

3) Clear and Concise

a) Just tell your story as it happened, as you know it. No embellishments, no assumptions, and never include your opinions.

b) When the specific subject of the story changes, such as going from a witness statement to a specific observation you have made, start a new paragraph.

c) Separate your paragraphs with a space. This keeps your reports easier to read.

d) Keep your notes and surveillance recordings for future reference; you will need them while testifying. Your firm should already have a policy in place for these issues.

e) Include at least one specific penal code charge for each arrest, and one specific store safety violation for each safety issue or accident reported.

f) Include suggested corrective action (for safety issues ONLY).

g) Attach copies of photos and original copy of inventories and witness statements.

h) Be prepared to disperse copies of your report to your Manager, Supervisor, and r other entities as your firm requires.

i) Keep a complete copy for your own records, along with your field notebook.

RECOVERED PROPERTY

When describing recovered or stolen property it is important to be accurate. It is equally important to use the correct wording, so as to not make sensational claims and potentially leave yourself open to a civil suit.

For example, when describing jewelry without a written and signed statement from the lawful owner containing their description, you should avoid using the following words:

1) GOLD

2) SILVER

3) PLATINUM

4) DIAMOND

5) RUBY, or any other specific gem stone

Instead, get in the habit of using the following terms to describe the same materials:

a) YELLOW METAL

b) WHITE METAL

c) CLEAR or WHITE CENTER PIECE or PIECES

d) ANY OTHER COLOR.

2) QUOTE the legal owner's statement of value whenever possible.(

a) Never state a value for an item without a copy of the price tag and SKU# if you do not have a written statement from the legal owner.

3) Include any distinguishing MARKINGS, DESIGNS and SERIAL NUMBERS (including any damage observed)

After photographing and cataloging your recovered property seal it in a clear 'zip lock' type clear, plastic bag and be ready to turn it over to law enforcement along with your detainee (if you have one).

Ideally, you should photograph any recovered items from a dorsal (top-down) view, with a ruler for size verification to the left of the item. If a ruler is unavailable you may substitute a quarter or dollar bill, as they are relatively universal in size and shape. This makes a solid enough reference as to the recovered item's estimated size and shape.

DESCRIBING MOTOR VEHICLES

On occasion you may have to describe a motor vehicle. For this, law enforcement report writing courses (including California P.O.S.T. courses) suggest memorizing the acronym C.Y.M.B.L., which stands for:

1) COLOR
2) YEAR
3) MAKE & MODEL
4) BODY STYLE
   a) SEDAN
   b) COUPE
   c) CONVERTIBLE
   d) PICK UP TRUCK
   e) ETC.
5) LICENSE PLATE
   a) VIN if known.
   b) OTHER DISTINGUISHING FEATURES
      i)   ROLL BARS
      ii) BUMPER STICKERS

DESCRIBING PEOPLE

When describing people, it helps to use the TOP-DOWN and OUTSIDE-IN methods.

1) Start at the head.

   a) HAT

   b) HAIR, FACIAL HAIR, GLASSES, ETC.

   c) INCLUDE COLOR, STYLE or CUT

2) DESCRIBE THE OUTERMOST GARMENT FIRST (OUTSIDE-IN, remember?)

   a) TYPE

   b) COLOR

   c) SLEEVE LENGTH

3) Now the legs

   a) PANTS

   b) SHORTS

   c) SKIRT

   d) INCLUDE COLOR, STYLE or CUT

4) Then the feet

   a) SHOES, SANDALS, BOOTS, ETC

   b) INCLUDE COLOR, STYLE or CUT

TESTIFYING IN COURT

Courtroom demeanor can make or break not only your case but your career. Your superiors will always take into account whether or not your cases lead to successful prosecutions and financial restitution.

Dress accordingly. Wear a suit and tie, or a conservative dress as you see fit, unless your department requires you to wear your full uniform in court. Courts are not the venue for expressing your individuality.

Remain respectful and professional in and out of the courtroom. Just because you are not on trial does not mean that you are not being judged. Unprofessional conduct or mannerisms can give an attorney ammunition to use to tear apart your character, which can reduce the chances of a conviction, and increase the odds of you and your department being sued for wrongful prosecution.

Restitution can be sued for from the people responsible for the theft, and if your report and testimony does not conclude in favor of your store you did not prevent a loss, you created one. Wear a suit and tie, or a conservative dress as your gender or personal preferences for civilian professional attire dictates.

Courts are not the venue for expressing your individuality. Show respect for the institution.

APPLICABLE CA PENAL CODES (Circa 2013)

CA PC 484 Petty theft (a) Every person who shall feloniously steal, take, carry, lead, or drive away the personal property of another, or who shall fraudulently appropriate property which has been entrusted to him or her, or who shall knowingly and designedly, by any false or fraudulent representation or pretense, defraud any other person of money, labor or real or personal property, or who causes or procures others to report falsely of his or her wealth or mercantile character and by thus imposing upon any person, obtains credit and thereby fraudulently gets or obtains possession of money, or property or obtains the labor or service of another, is guilty of theft. In determining the value of the property obtained, for the purposes of this section, the reasonable and fair market value shall be the test, and in determining the value of services received the contract price shall be the test. If there be no contract price, the reasonable and going wage for the service rendered shall govern. For the purposes of this section, any false or fraudulent representation or pretense made shall be treated as continuing, so as to cover any money, property or service received as a result thereof, and the complaint, information or indictment may charge that the crime was committed on any date during the particular period in question. The hiring of any additional employee or employees without advising each of them of every labor claim due and unpaid and every judgment that the employer has been unable to meet shall be prima facie evidence of intent to defraud.

CA PC 459 Every person who enters any house, room, apartment, tenement, shop, warehouse, store, mill, barn, stable, outhouse or other building, tent, vessel, as defined in Section 21 of the Harbors and Navigation Code, floating home, as defined in subdivision (d) of Section 18075.55 of the Health and Safety Code, railroad car, locked or sealed cargo container, whether or not mounted on a vehicle, trailer coach, as defined in Section 635 of the Vehicle Code, any house car, as defined in Section 362 of the Vehicle Code, inhabited camper, as defined in Section 243 of the Vehicle Code, vehicle as defined by the Vehicle Code, when the doors are locked, aircraft as defined by Section 21012 of the Public Utilities Code, or mine or any underground portion thereof, with intent to commit grand or petit larceny or any felony is guilty of burglary. As used in this chapter, inhabited means currently being used for dwelling purposes, whether occupied or not. A house, trailer, vessel designed for habitation, or portion of a building is currently being used for dwelling purposes if, at the time of the burglary, it was not occupied solely because a natural or other disaster caused the occupants to leave the premises.

CA PC 460 (a) Every burglary of an inhabited dwelling house, vessel, as defined in the Harbors and Navigation Code, which is inhabited and designed for habitation, floating home, as defined in subdivision (d) of Section 18075.55 of the Health and Safety Code, or trailer coach, as defined by the Vehicle Code, or the inhabited portion of any other building, is burglary of the first degree. (b) All other kinds of burglary are of the second degree. (c) This section shall not be construed to supersede or affect Section 464 of the Penal Code.

CA PC 464 Any person who, with intent to commit crime, enters, either by day or by night, any building, whether inhabited or not, and opens or attempts to open any vault, safe, or other secure place by use of acetylene torch or electric arc, burning bar, thermal lance, oxygen lance, or any other similar device capable of burning through steel, concrete, or any other solid substance, or by use of nitroglycerine, dynamite, gunpowder, or any other explosive, is guilty of a felony and, upon conviction, shall be punished by imprisonment in the state prison for a term of three, five, or seven years.

CA PC 666 (a) Notwithstanding Section 490, every person who, having been convicted three or more times of petty theft, grand theft, auto theft under Section 10851 of the Vehicle Code, burglary, carjacking, robbery, or a felony violation of Section 496 and having served a term therefore in any penal institution or having been imprisoned therein as a condition of probation for that offense, is subsequently convicted of petty theft, then the person convicted of that subsequent offense is punishable by imprisonment in the county jail not exceeding one year, or in the state prison. (b) Notwithstanding Section 490, any person described in paragraph (1) who, having been convicted of petty theft, grand theft, auto theft under Section 10851 of the Vehicle Code, burglary, carjacking, robbery, or a felony violation of Section 496, and having served a term of imprisonment therefore in any penal institution or having been imprisoned therein as a condition of probation for that offense, who is subsequently convicted of petty theft, is punishable by imprisonment in the county jail not exceeding one year, or in the state prison. This subdivision shall apply to any person who is required to register pursuant to the Sex Offender Registration Act, or who has a prior violent or serious felony conviction, as specified in subdivision (c) of Section 667.5 or subdivision (c) of Section 1192.7. This subdivision shall not be construed to preclude prosecution or punishment pursuant to subdivisions (b) to (i), inclusive, of Section 667, or Section 1170.12.